RosaParks

CHRISTINE TAYLOR-BUTLER

Children's Press®
An Imprint of Scholastic Inc.
New York Toronto London Auckland Sydney
Mexico City New Delhi Hong Kong
Danbury, Connecticut

Content Consultant
James Marten, PhD
Professor and Chair, History Department
Marquette University
Milwaukee, Wisconsin

Library of Congress Cataloging-in-Publication Data
Taylor-Butler, Christine.
 Rosa Parks / by Christine Taylor-Butler.
    pages cm. — (A true book)
 Includes bibliographical references and index.
 ISBN 978-0-531-21195-3 (library binding : alk. paper) — ISBN 978-0-531-21209-7 (pbk. : alk. paper)
1. Parks, Rosa, 1913–2005—Juvenile literature. 2. African American women—Alabama—
Montgomery—Biography—Juvenile literature. 3. African Americans—Alabama—Montgomery—
Biography—Juvenile literature. 4. Civil rights workers—Alabama—Montgomery—Biography—
Juvenile literature. 5. African Americans—Civil rights—Alabama—Montgomery—History—20th
century—Juvenile literature. 6. Segregation in transportation—Alabama—Montgomery—
History—20th century—Juvenile literature. 7. Montgomery (Ala.) —Race relations—Juvenile lit-
erature. 8. Montgomery (Ala.) —Biography—Juvenile literature. I. Title.
 F334.M753T49 2015
 323.092—dc23 [B]   2014031011

**Front cover: Parks sitting on a
bus in Montgomery, Alabama**

**Back cover: Parks's mug shot
from her 1955 arrest**

Find the Truth!

Everything you are about to read is true *except* for one of the sentences on this page.

Which one is **TRUE**?

T or F Rosa Parks was the first woman arrested on a bus.

T or F Rosa Parks received more than two dozen honorary doctorate degrees.

Find the answers in this book.

3

Contents

THE **BIG** TRUTH!

The Women Behind the Bus Boycott

7053

Rosa Parks's arrest sparked a bus boycott.

Parks started a foundation to help students.

Rosa Parks was working as a seamstress at the time she became famous.

CHAPTER 1

Strong Willed From the Start

Rosa Louise McCauley was born on February 4, 1913. Her father, James McCauley, was a carpenter. Her mother, Leona McCauley, was a teacher. The family, including Rosa's younger brother, Sylvester, lived in a small house in Tuskegee, Alabama.

Little did the McCauleys know that their Rosa would grow up to be a strong **advocate** for **civil rights**. She would also make history.

 Rosa Parks is known as the "Mother of Civil Rights."

Living Under Jim Crow

Rosa's parents separated when Rosa was only two years old. She moved with her mother and brother to her grandparents' farm in Pine Level, Alabama. But life in Alabama was not easy. At that time, Jim Crow laws dictated that whites and blacks had separate public facilities, such as schools, hospitals, bathrooms, and restaurant and theater seating. This was known as **segregation**. Even the drinking fountains were separate. Rosa often wondered what "white" water tasted like.

A child drinks from a segregated water fountain.

Jim Crow was the name of a black character depicted by a white actor in dark makeup.

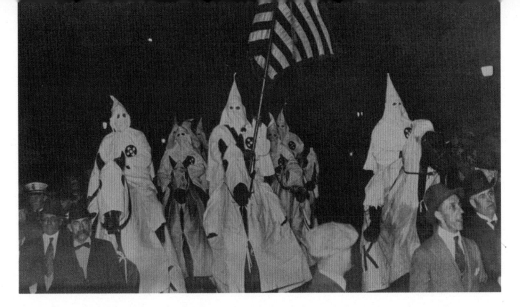

Members of the Ku Klux Klan wore long robes and hoods that covered their faces.

In the first half of the 20th century, acts of violence against minorities were common, and black people often lived in fear. The Ku Klux Klan was a secret and often brutal organization that opposed equal rights for minorities. Rosa's grandfather remembered what it was like to be mistreated. He had worked on a plantation where he was beaten and starved as a boy. Each night during Rosa's childhood, he sat on the porch to protect the family as the Ku Klux Klan marched past their house.

Black students had to walk to school, no matter what school they attended or where it was located.

Growing Up

Because Rosa was small for her age and often sick with **tonsillitis**, her mother homeschooled her. But Rosa protested. At age nine, Rosa finally had her tonsils removed, which ended the tonsillitis. Soon after, Rosa's mother allowed her to attend a school run by a local church.

Rosa experienced mistreatment on her way to and from school. Black children had to walk to school no matter the distance. White children on buses taunted Rosa and other children as they walked by.

Rosa was strong-willed and not afraid to stand up for herself. When someone pushed her, she pushed back. But her mother worked to teach her to control her anger. Remaining calm would allow her to think and act effectively. Rosa followed her mother's advice. She even developed a reputation as a Goody Two-Shoes.

When Rosa was 11 years old, she enrolled at Miss White's School for Girls in Montgomery, Alabama. She studied English, science, geography, cooking, and sewing.

Miss White's School for Girls was a private school run by women from the northern states.

There were no public high schools for black students in Montgomery. When it came time for high school, Rosa attended a laboratory school at Alabama State Teachers College for Negroes. A laboratory school is a school for experimenting with new teaching methods or for training new teachers. However, Rosa's grandmother became very ill. In 1929, Rosa left school to care for her. After her grandmother died, Rosa's mother became ill. Rosa stayed home to become her caregiver.

Segregation limited the black population's access to schools, particularly in the South.

Jim Crow Laws

Jim Crow laws were enacted beginning in the late 1800s. Under such laws, black people could not eat in the same restaurant as white people. They could not work the same jobs, use the same seats on public transportation, or be buried in the same area of a cemetery. Even the bathrooms and drinking fountains were separated by race. Jim Crow was outlawed in 1964 after Congress passed the Civil Rights Act.

WAITING ROOM
FOR WHITE ONLY

BY ORDER
POLICE DEPT.

It was through her husband, Raymond, that Rosa first became active and outspoken in the movement for civil rights.

N.A.A.C.P.
MEETING
←

Becoming Rosa Parks

In 1931, a friend introduced Rosa to Raymond Parks, a local barber. He worked at Maxwell Air Force Base in Montgomery. Raymond was self-educated and as a child had taught himself to read. In fact, he was so smart that people thought he had gone to college. Rosa was shy and refused to date him at first. But she liked his personality and his strength.

 NAACP stands for National Association for the Advancement of Colored People.

**Raymond drove a red Nash. It was
rare for a black person to own a car.**

Changes and Challenges

Raymond was an **activist**. An activist is someone
who works to change rules and laws that are
unjust. During dates together, Rosa and Raymond
would sit in his car and have long talks about
ways to improve life for black people. Rosa
married Raymond on December 18, 1932. He
encouraged her to complete her education. He
knew it was important to her. Rosa received her
high school diploma in 1934.

Raymond volunteered with the National Association for the Advancement of Colored People (NAACP). The group sometimes held meetings in the Parks's home. During the 1930s, Raymond helped the NAACP work to save nine young black men known as the Scottsboro Boys. They had been falsely accused of violently attacking two white women and were sentenced to death. Raymond did not want Rosa involved. It was dangerous. Activists often received threats of violence. Rosa feared for Raymond's life.

Charges were eventually dropped for four of the Scottsboro Boys. All nine were pardoned in 2013, long after their deaths.

Taking Action

As Raymond worked with the NAACP, Rosa wanted to get involved, too. Because of her race, she had trouble finding work that fit her skills. She eventually found work as a seamstress at a department store. Rosa refused to use the segregated water fountains or bathrooms. Her brother had been **drafted** into the army, but state and local laws prevented him from voting when he returned home. All these injustices motivated Rosa to take action.

A sign at a bus terminal indicates the direction to the waiting room reserved for black travelers.

ONE WORLD – *OR NONE*

The NAACP was founded in 1909.

The NAACP, like many organizations at the time, was dominated by male membership.

In 1943, Rosa attended her first NAACP meeting. She was the only woman present. During the meeting, she took detailed notes. The men immediately elected her secretary of the Montgomery chapter of the NAACP. That same year, Rosa tried to register to vote but was not granted a voting card. She was also thrown off a bus for refusing to use the back door. She grew angry but remembered not to show her emotion.

Edgar Nixon (center) became an important force in the fight for civil rights.

Things changed when Rosa Parks met Pullman porter Edgar Nixon. Pullman porters served white passengers on the sleeping cars of trains. They had been an early force in the fight for better pay and treatment of black workers. On his travels, Nixon had seen black and white people eating and working together. He wanted to see this occur in Montgomery, too. He became president of the Montgomery NAACP chapter and teamed up with Parks.

Discrimination and registration clerks made it nearly impossible for black people to register to vote. Without registering, they could not vote. In order to register, people took a test. Black people were given harder tests than white people. In 1945, Parks made a third attempt to register. Parks knew her test answers were correct. She copied them on a separate sheet of paper as proof. Afraid she might file a lawsuit, the clerk let her pass.

In some areas, black people needed a white person to vouch for them to register to vote.

Segregated citizens in Tennessee wait in lines to register to vote.

The Women Behind the Bus Boycott

Rosa Parks was one of many women fighting to end discrimination. Long before the men of the NAACP became involved, the Women's Political Council (WPC) was pressuring the city government in Montgomery to end bus segregation. They demanded the bus company hire black drivers. The WPC also distributed leaflets to inform the community when women were being jailed for refusing to give up their seats. They finally urged people to organize and boycott buses. Without women, the bus boycott might not have happened.

Jo Ann Robinson, president of the WPC, was arrested for her role in the bus boycott in Montgomery.

Women lead a group of protesters during Montgomery's bus boycott.

A protester is carried out of a public library after trying to protest the library's policy of segregation.

CHAPTER 3

The Last Straw

In 1954, Parks started an NAACP youth group for teens. She worked with the teens to plan a protest at the local library. The library did not allow black people to borrow books. Because activists were often threatened, beaten, or even killed, many families were afraid to send their children to the meetings. Fifteen-year-old Claudette Colvin was one of the few teens to join the group.

Black protesters staged "Read-ins" at whites-only libraries to protest segregated libraries.

Claudette Takes on Buses

Everyone entered a public bus through the front door to pay the same fare. White passengers could then find a seat. Jim Crow laws required black passengers to leave and enter again through the back door. Black people could not sit next to or across from a white person. Seats toward the front were reserved for white people. If the white seats became full, black passengers had to move farther back so that white passengers could sit.

Sometimes buses left before black passengers could walk to the back door to enter the bus. Sometimes buses passed by them without stopping.

Claudette Colvin was found guilty of three charges, but two were later dropped.

Parks helped raise money for Claudette's defense.

In March 1955, a bus driver ordered Claudette to give her seat to a white passenger. She refused. Normally, she would have been thrown off the bus for that. This time, she was arrested.

The WPC was planning a bus boycott and was looking for an incident to use as a way to gain public attention and support. The NAACP did not think enough people would rally around the teenager, so the boycott was put on hold.

A Fight Begins

Another teenager, Mary Louise Smith, was arrested on October 1. Even so, the NAACP waited to boycott.

Then on December 1, 1955, Parks boarded a bus and sat in the first row reserved for "colored" people. Every other seat was filled. The bus driver demanded that black passengers stand in the aisle to make room for a white man. Three people stood up. Parks scooted closer to the window.

Timeline of the Life of Rosa Parks

December 18, 1932

Rosa McCauley marries Raymond Parks.

February 4, 1913

Rosa Louise McCauley is born.

1945

Rosa Parks successfully registers to vote in Alabama.

The city of Montgomery had given its bus drivers certain police powers. The driver, James Blake, carried a gun and could arrest Parks. But Parks was tired of being pushed around. She was tired of being treated like a second-class citizen. The city code said she could keep her seat if no others were available. When the driver asked Parks if she was going to stand up, she said, "No. I am not."

December 5, 1955

The Montgomery bus boycott begins.

December 1, 1955

Parks is arrested after refusing to give up her seat on a bus.

Parks knew the police had mistreated Claudette Colvin when they arrested her the previous year. She knew the same thing might happen to her. Even so, when Blake threatened to call the police, Parks said quietly, "Go ahead." Blake called for help at a pay phone. When the police arrived, they seemed reluctant to make the arrest. They knew the NAACP might become involved. Blake insisted on pressing charges.

A police officer takes Parks's fingerprints.

The police took this booking photo of Parks for their files when she was arrested.

Parks was thrown in jail and charged with violating Section 11 of the Montgomery city code. Edgar Nixon paid $100 **bail** for her release. Clifford Durr, a white civil rights lawyer, went with him to vouch for Parks. Nixon told Parks that the NAACP wanted to use her arrest to jump-start the bus boycott. Raymond Parks disagreed with the plan. He was afraid his wife would face violence. Rosa hesitated. Nixon persisted until she said yes.

The Bus Boycott

In court, the **prosecutors** realized that Rosa Parks had not violated the city code. They asked the judge to change the charge to reflect a violation of the state code. Parks's lawyer objected. Even so, the judge agreed with the prosecutors. Parks was convicted and fined $10, plus $4 in court costs.

Attorney Fred Gray offered to file an appeal of Parks's conviction for free.

Rosa Parks earned only $25 a week as a seamstress in Montgomery.

Martin Luther King Jr. was one of the leaders who took part in the Montgomery bus boycott.

Making Plans

On December 5, 1955, a rally was held to organize a Montgomery bus boycott. Thousands of people showed up at the Holt Street Baptist Church for the meeting. Edgar Nixon spoke first. Then he introduced a new speaker, 26-year-old Martin Luther King Jr. People in the audience wanted to hear from Parks, too. Parks sat on the stage with the men, but they did not allow her to speak.

That night, the Montgomery Improvement Association (MIA) was formed. The MIA organized carpools and taxis for boycott participants. People were charged 10 cents for a ride, the same as the bus charged. As the boycott got going, participants flashed a "V" for victory sign to show they were part of the cause. Women formed the backbone of the boycott. They held bake sales and fund-raisers. They walked miles to work as empty buses passed by.

More than 300 cars joined the boycott carpool.

Challenges and Victories

There were consequences. Sugar was poured in carpool gas tanks. Acid was thrown at participating cars. People received threats at home and at work. Because of the boycott, Parks lost her job at the department store. Her husband lost his job on the military base. Parks began traveling around the country to give speeches and to raise awareness. She raised a lot of money for the cause.

During the boycott, the use of Montgomery buses dropped by 90 percent.

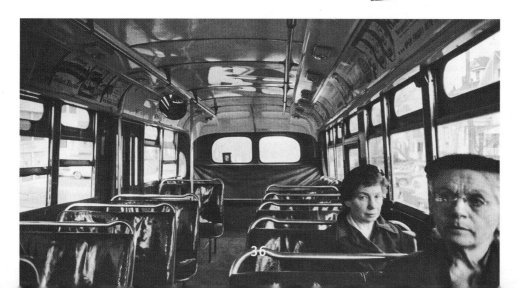

Parks and a fellow boycotter sit at the front of a bus to celebrate the end of segregation on buses.

The Montgomery bus company was forced to raise fares and lay off bus drivers. But they would not change their rules. The city of Montgomery refused to budge as well.

On June 19, 1956, a federal district court ruled that bus segregation was **unconstitutional**. On November 13, 1956, the Supreme Court agreed. Soon after, Parks rode on her first desegregated bus. The boycott had lasted 381 days.

Parks traveled widely over the years in support of civil rights movements around the world.

CHAPTER 5

A Light in the Darkness

Rosa could not find work after the boycott, even with the organizations with which she had worked on the bus boycott. Unemployed and facing threats of violence because of their participation in the bus boycott, Rosa and Raymond Parks moved to Detroit, Michigan, where they could start over. In 1965, Rosa began working for Congressman John Conyers. She continued working for him until she retired in 1988.

 Parks traveled around the world to talk about civil rights.

Rosa Parks reads a book she helped write about her work to a group of children at the opening of an after-school program.

Parks's husband liked her hair long. She never cut it, even after he died.

Working for the Future

Raymond Parks died in 1977. He and Rosa never had children. Ten years later, Rosa created the Rosa and Raymond Parks Institute for Self Development. Her goal was to offer scholarships to help students in Detroit pursue their future dreams. It also offered courses in communication, political awareness, and health. She wanted to help young people develop a sense of hope, dignity, and pride.

People around the world honored Rosa Parks's contributions to freedom. Statues were erected in her honor, and she received more than two dozen honorary doctorate degrees. In 1994, she traveled to Sweden to receive the Rosa Parks Peace Prize. The committee that awarded the prize called Parks "a light in the darkness." In 1996, she was awarded the Presidential Medal of Freedom. In 1999, she received the U.S. Congressional Gold Medal.

Parks gives a speech after receiving the Congressional Gold Medal.

Rosa Parks died on October 24, 2005. Black ribbons were placed on the front seats of buses in Montgomery and Detroit. Her body was sent to Washington, D.C., to lie in honor at the U.S. Capitol Rotunda. More than 50,000 people stood in line to pay their respects.

On the day of her funeral, President George W. Bush ordered all U.S. flags to be flown at half-mast in respect.

Parks was the first woman and second African American to lie in honor in the Capitol Rotunda.

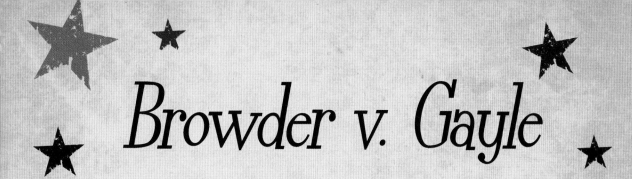

Browder v. Gayle

Although Parks's arrest ignited the bus boycott, a different lawsuit ended bus segregation. Five women—Aurelia Browder, Susie McDonald, Claudette Colvin, Mary Louise Smith, and Jeanette Reese—had been arrested before Parks. Fred Gray, who also acted as Parks's lawyer, filed a lawsuit in their names against Montgomery mayor W. A. Gayle. In 1956, three judges ruled that the segregation of buses deprived the women of the equal protection guaranteed by the 14th Amendment. ★

Amendment that established African Americans' right to vote: 15th Amendment, 1870

Year school segregation was declared constitutional: 1896

Year that school segregation was declared unconstitutional: 1954

Year bus segregation was declared unconstitutional: 1956

Year the Civil Rights Act was passed: 1964

Year the Voting Rights Act was passed: 1965

Did you find the truth?

(F) Rosa Parks was the first woman arrested on a bus.

(T) Rosa Parks received more than two dozen honorary doctorate degrees.

Resources

Books

Aretha, David. *The Story of Rosa Parks and the Montgomery Bus Boycott in Photographs*. Berkeley Heights, NJ: Enslow, 2014.

Kittinger, Jo S., and Stephen Walker. *Rosa's Bus*. Honesdale, PA: Calkins Creek, 2010.

Visit this Scholastic Web site for more information on Rosa Parks:
★ www.factsfornow.scholastic.com
Enter the keywords **Rosa Parks**

Important Words

activist (AK-tiv-ist) — a person who works for some kind of social change

advocate (AD-vuh-kit) — a person who supports an idea or plan

bail (BAYL) — money paid to a court for the release of someone accused of a crime, with the promise that he or she will show up for the trial

civil rights (SIV-uhl RITES) — the individual rights that all members of a democratic society have to freedom and equal treatment under the law

discrimination (diss-crim-uh-NAY-shun) — unfair treatment of others based on age, race, gender, or other factors

drafted (DRAF-tid) — made to join the armed forces

prosecutors (PRAH-sih-kyoo-turz) — lawyers who try a person for a crime

segregation (seg-ruh-GAY-shuhn) — the act of separating people based on race, gender, or other factors

tonsillitis (tahn-suh-LYE-tis) — an illness that makes a person's tonsils, or the flaps of skin that lie on each side of the throat, infected and painful

unconstitutional (uhn-kahn-sti-TOO-shuh-nuhl) — not in keeping with the basic principles or laws set forth in the constitution of a state or country

Index

Page numbers in **bold** indicate illustrations.

About the Author

Christine Taylor-Butler is the author of more than 75 books for children including the True Book series on American history and government, health and the human body, and science experiments. A graduate of the Massachusetts Institute of Technology, Christine holds degrees in both civil engineering and art and design. She currently lives in Kansas City, Missouri.